a pocketful of sequins

WORDS FROM THE HEART

Published by Moonstone Media
65 Hume St
Crows Nest NSW 2065 Australia

First produced by Moonstone Media 2006
Text copyright © NBCF
Illustrations copyright © Julianne Lord

Cover and text design by Natalie Edwards

Illustrations by Julianne Lord

Produced by Moonstone Media
Moonstone Media was born from the belief that books
can make a difference in the world. From conception to
completion Moonstone creates books for individuals or
companies who share this philosophy. By focusing on
selective projects, the unique needs of each client and
creative collaboration, Moonstone proudly shares its
vision of a world made better by books.

Proudly supported by Macquarie Bank Foundation

Macquarie Bank
Foundation

ISBN 0977559904
Printed in China

MOONSTONE MEDIA

These key national breast cancer organisations work separately and together to improve breast cancer outcomes through:

- ↬ high quality and coordinated research into treatments, care and ultimately a cure
- ↬ evidence-based, quality information and improved care for those affected, their families and their health care professionals
- ↬ access to decision-makers and support for those who have trodden the same path

The **National Breast Cancer Foundation** is the leading Australian national not-for-profit organisation promoting and investing in high quality and coordinated research into treatments, care and ultimately prevention

NATIONAL
BREAST CANCER FOUNDATION
FUNDING RESEARCH FOR PREVENTION AND CURE

Breast Cancer Network Australia
empowers, informs, represents and links together Australians personally affected by breast cancer

Breast
Cancer
Network
Australia

The **National Breast Cancer Centre** is funded by the Australian Government to improve outcomes for women with breast and ovarian cancer through the translation of research into evidence-based information, education and awareness

NATIONAL BREAST CANCER CENTRE
incorporating the Ovarian Cancer Program

Most women who are diagnosed with breast cancer will be treated successfully. But, sadly, 2,700 women in Australia still lose their lives to breast cancer every year.

The words in this book were spoken by women across the spectrum of this experience and, occasionally, their family and friends. Some of the quotes are joyful, some philosophical, others exquisitely poignant. Their diversity reflects the limitless ways in which courage, humour and strength are revealed in the face of challenge.

Proceeds from A Pocketful of Sequins will be used by Australia's three national breast cancer organisations to fund initiatives to improve outcomes for women with breast cancer through research, support and information.

For the women and men who have lost their lives to breast cancer.

my body may be damaged
but not my spirit
my breasts may be gone
but not my laughter
my hair may fall
but not my hope
fear may grip
but gentle hands caress
faith may desert me
but family surround me
tears may flow
but so does love
my cleavage may no longer exist
but I do!

happiness is...
having one jiggly breast
and one non-jiggly breast
that still look great
in a beautiful dress.

Di 59

what a beautiful thing

it is to lose
your inhibitions
and speak
and live
by your heart.

Noel 64

I no longer fear anything in this world

even my scars are beautiful,

because my beauty is my respect for myself.

remember me as someone who...
lived with heart; took the time to listen; had a sense
of humour and a sense of self; woke up happy in
her partner's arms and ran naked under a full moon.

Stephanie   44

if you can help one person to travel her journey with
a little more ease, you have done good in the world.

Maxine 57

someone asked me,

'did you have all your nymph glands removed?'

that's LYMPH glands, I said.

they can take my breasts but they will never take my libido!

Karen 42

there is nothing more
beautiful than seeing an
elderly couple caring for
each other.

Lillian   70

I once saw a woman
put mascara on her
one remaining eyelash.
and in that moment,
I understood the true meaning
of beauty.

Lexie   41

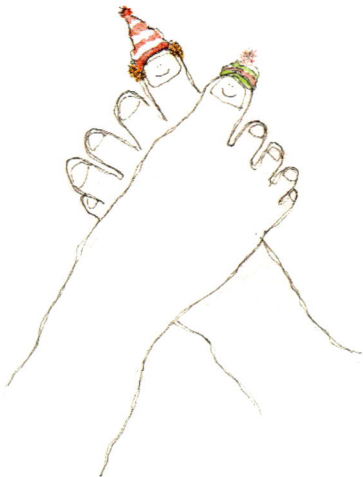

love your children. be passionate
about life. make others feel good
about themselves. and don't take
life too seriously - it's exhausting.

Lee   48

in this life,
it is worth having a good heart
and a musical instrument.

Catherine 46

even

in

the

depths

of

fear,

people

sparkle

with

courage.

Dorrine 66

stop and appreciate a
hug from your child,
an embrace from your
husband, reading to
your kids, a funny
joke. in those
moments we are
experiencing the best
of what life offers.

Danielle 41

when you get bad news,
it is not the end of the
world. you can make
anything into a beginning.

Lillian   70

work less. play more. love harder.

Marie   43

if I was told
I had one month
left to live,
I'd go to italy
to paint
and
potter around.
I wouldn't rush.
I would linger
in
beautiful spaces,
take my time in
places that I love and
drink lots of
red wine.

Margie 53

I tread on this earth as lightly as I can to make

the least impact - I hope that when I'm gone,

people I know will only miss me as much as

a warm evening breeze that once caressed

their faces.

Mary   53

if you want to experience real happiness,
hold your grandchildren close.
listen to what they say.

Anne 66

coming of age

the day my mother turned forty
we took her home from hospital
tenderly
gingerly
and without her breasts.

I was fifteen.

when she took a bath
she needed me;
she could not wash herself.

I did not want to be in that small room
shut in with those two red scars
strangling her chest
and sharpening their teeth on my green charity.

what I wanted was purple eye-liner
a lurex boob-tube
and scott gladesbrook at the cinema.

instead, I washed my mother's back
and helped her from the bath
tenderly
gingerly
without her breasts.

it takes courage to pick up the phone
when the person you're calling is
doing it tough.

Di 59

learn from six-year olds. six-year olds
don't worry about anything or have any
rules. they jump in puddles, blow
bubbles, make sand castles, laugh.
they know how to be free.

Robyn 47

there is nothing more beautiful than the blue eyes of my 12-week old granddaughter, which never leave my face when I talk to her.

Leonie 61

the best thing
to say to someone
who is suffering
or in pain is,

'I know, my darling, it sucks.'

Lee 48

In this life, it is worth having at least one Italian lover who thinks you're the most beautiful woman in the world!!

Marie 54

when
I
am
useful
to
others,
I
am
strong.

Susan 54

courage is showing one's face

in public when one feels

like a plucked chook.

without a hair on one's head

not an eyelash or eyebrow. but with a smile on one's face.

Helen 59

Remember me for
my open door
the calm I brought to a crisis
my nose for a bargain
my pink feather boa
in a chemo ward.
remember me as someone
who did not fade into the walls.

Judith   49

each day

in its wondrous

variety brings moments

of joy -

a lightning storm

a cluster of wildflowers

the boys getting their L-plates

the smell of a fresh morning

catching a wave to the shore

floating effortlessly in the

crystal blue water.....

Sharon   44

courage is not
about climbing mount everest.
people are heroes
in what they do in their everyday
lives when they take a leap of faith
without a safety net.

Allan 38

live everyday.
do things
that make your heart sing...
and stuff
the housework!!

Catherine   42

my little boy
looked under my scarf
at my bald head
and said,
'Oh mummy, you look really handsome.'
my four-year old's way of telling me
in his eyes
I was beautiful
still.

Suellen   46

beauty

is a verb
not a noun.
and it's going
on around us,
at every moment.
even now.

Annie   41

It is more important for my sons to remember me sitting on the beach, glass of wine in hand, watching them surf as the sun sets, than in a sterile home full of beds made, dishes done, squeaky clean windows and mopped floors.

Marlene 48

it

does not matter what you say
to someone who is suffering.
it only matters that you
are there and speak
from the heart.

Kerry 59

a smile

is the most beautiful and
multi-lingual silent statement.
a smile can mean
so many things:
hello
I'm so happy
guess what I've been doing?
I am a friend
thanks
pleased to meet you
no one can tell I'm in pain
everything will be all right
it's great to see you back on your feet and looking so well
I'm here if you need a hug.

Jan 50

when someone is in pain,
offer to hold her hand.
nothing more.

Doreen   61

COOK

with love, look into people's eyes, be open to life's lessons, have lots of fun and laugh your head off. *Lee 48*

life

here

on

earth

is

temporary.

therefore, so

is suffering.

Jenny 48

beauty is...

a friend's hair growing back

Jan 50

i
have learned to
shrug my shoulders
at the trivia that so
many people agonise
over.
and
I sleep so much better
because of it.

Anne   66

courage is doing what is right for you
when no-one else thinks it is.

Stephanie 44

these days

I spend more money on things
that bring me joy - I look in
the mirror and smile and I
stop to watch dogs bark at water.

I have become less careless of each day.

if I am asked for lunch, or to meet a friend,

I do it if I possibly can.

I try never to find a reason to say no.

Anne 66

always assume you are going
to lose the people you love
tomorrow. and act on
that assumption
today

Greg 50

it is an act of generosity to
accept the help of others.
it restores both the giver
and the receiver.

Marina 46

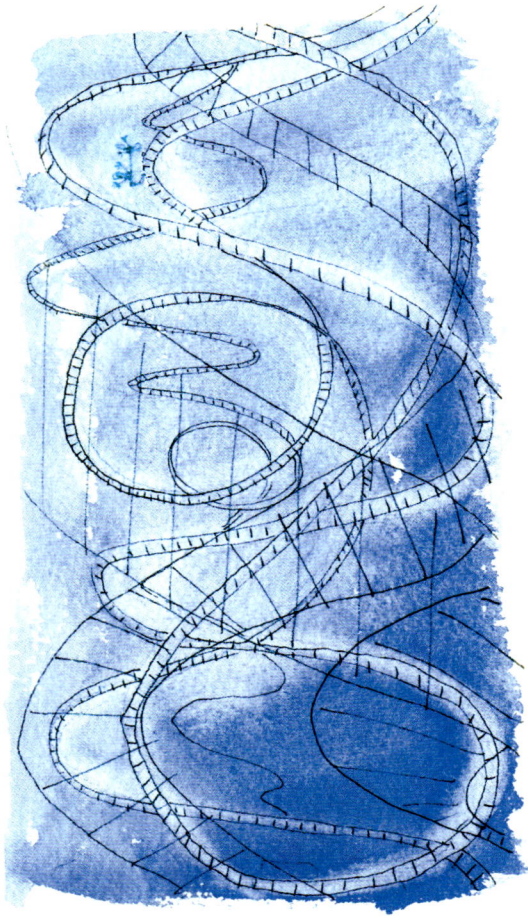

don't spurn
the hard lessons.
what you lose in naiveté,
you gain in insight.

Annie 41

in this world of greed and
self-obsession, I am moved by
the beauty of individual women
facing adversity with courage.

Dr Paul   63

if you say you're going to do something, do it.
don't put off what you've undertaken to do.

Sharon 44

give to others until it hurts.

but choose carefully
those to whom you give.

Marie 43

accept

confronting memories from the past.   they remind us
how far we have travelled since that time.

Marina 46

when people say
my son looks like her,
I search his face to find her there.

Greg   50

I
of little faith,
am deeply
touched
when a friend
asks if she
can pray for me,
and another
quietly admits
he has lit
a candle for me.
how precious
those blessings are.

Anne 66

breast cancer gave me a chance to have an affair with myself. I don't belong to any religious or social group. I belong to myself.

Jamal 47

love is ..

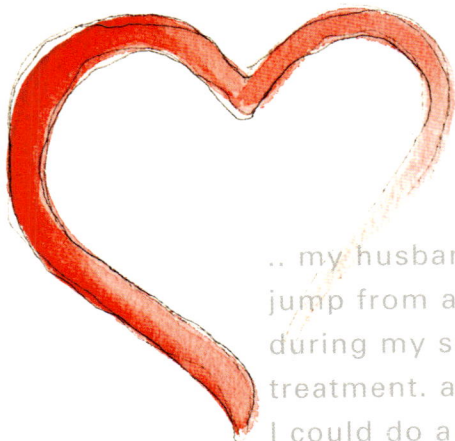

.. my husband arranging for me to
jump from a plane at 10 000 feet
during my six weeks of radiation
treatment. after I did that, I knew
I could do anything I wanted.

Yvonne 53

tell people you love
how important they
are. even if they
already know it,
tell them again.

Amanda 47

laughter gets you through
the hard times. I wanted to
write on the back of my
bald head: shit happens.

Robyn   47

I'd like to be remembered
as the person who
tried to do that
extra thing.
who put her hand
up when she
could.

Jennifer   42

poem for john

the doctor gave me the news.
there must be some mistake.
breast cancer? surely not me?

'hold on tight' you said,
'and we'll travel this path together.'

you fed me chilled watermelon,
piece by piece, morsel by morsel,
to cool my body from the chemo heat.

the medication made me fat.
I lost all my hair.
but you touched my face,
and told me I am the most
beautiful woman you've ever met.

you never really liked tattoos.
but the six dots on my chest
guide the radiation
that healed my body.

'wear them like medals' you said.
scarred forever, but not wounded.
we held on tight and travelled the path.
each day now we celebrate the life
of one more cancer survivor.

an infinite gap remains

of the things left unsaid

where her memory is left to die.

but I remember her wonder.

Elizabeth   13

sometimes fear
        and
            courage walk side by side.

Catherine   42

when you are suffering,
open your heart to accepting help
from family and friends. they too are hurting.

I don't know
what I'd say if
I had a chance
to say something
to my mum.
I guess
that if her spirit
is here,
then she
already knows.

Mark 10

face your worst fear
with calmness and balance.
beyond the fear, lies a true
appreciation for life,
a euphoria and an exhilaration
that comes from having
survived a challenging journey

Elizabeth   48

take a chance.

step outside
your comfort zone.
give it a try.

don't wonder
'what if?'

Jenny 43

all of us are born and all of us die.
if it is your time to go,
let it be a peaceful journey.

Jamal   47

sometimes suffering
brings us the
freedom and confidence
to make bold choices
about how
we want to live
the rest of our lives.

Maxine   57

late at night

I sit outside in the dark and
listen to the night sounds
no phone ringing
no emails to answer

just silence and
the night and

I am free

Anne   66

how would I like

to be remembered?

for my smile.

my wit.

and my taste in shoes.

Lexie 41

I have lost the need to be such a private person
and gained the strength to be vulnerable.

Helen 59

believe in the power of your spirit.

believe in inspiring people with who you are.

when you tell your story from a place of passion,

people cannot fail but to be moved.

Chris   41

change
the
things
you
can
control
and
walk
away
from
those
you
can't.

Karen 48

goals matter

not only for future happiness.
the journey towards them can
help us to feel better every day.

Domini 54

keep those who

are important to

you as close as

possible - not

necessarily to

your front door,

but to your heart.

Jennifer   42

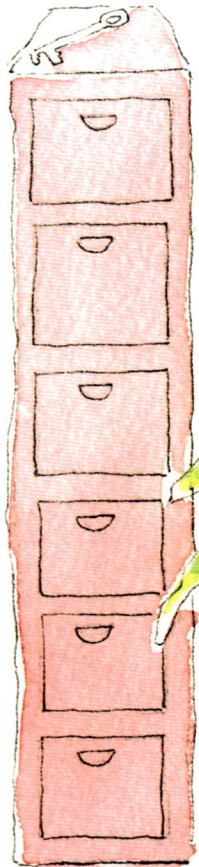

put your past in a filing cabinet.
take it out every so often and
have a look at it. but leave it
in the filing cabinet. it's too
heavy to lug around day by day.

Di 59

there is a necklace that
belongs to my mum with
a gold cross on it. dad
says that when I'm
responsible, I can wear it.

Mark 10

don't forgo
opportunities
because of pride.
learn to say,
'yes, thank you,'
and open your
hand to accept
what is offered. *Marlene 48*

stay in touch with people
who mean something to you.
meet for a cuppa.
pick up the phone.
flick an email.
don't just let time slip away.

Sharon   44

when someone
is in pain
ask her
'would you
like to talk
while I listen.'

Marie 54

dare to question.

cause chaos wherever it is needed.

do something to make the journey

for others a little easier.

Robyn   58

if

you're looking for things

to count, count your

blessings, not your problems.

Jennifer 42

suffering is inevitable, misery is optional.

cancer
eludes definition.
triumph? loss?
to some, perhaps.
only in my dreams
does language not matter
only feelings
where hearts connect
and go far beyond
the meaning of words.

Elizabeth   13

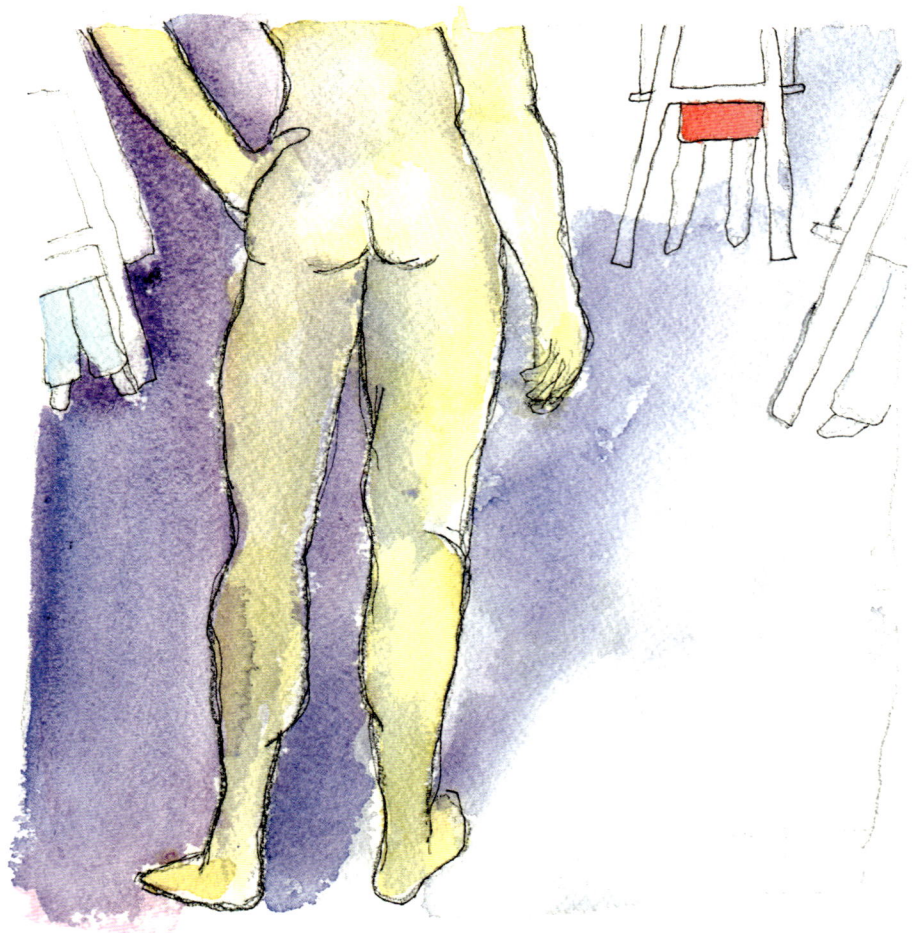

when you change the way you view life,
it changes the way others around you view it too.

Karen 48

take one day at a time but live it like there
is no tomorrow.

Robyn   58

every day
is a gift to
be opened
and *joy*

exclaimed
over!

Kerry 59

suffering brings its gifts.

it offers you the chance to experience

yourself at the deepest level.

Suellen 46

life is short.
drink only french champagne!

Annie 41

my body

may be

lopsided

but

my life

is well

balanced.

Jackie 59

give

your

hugs

freely

even

to

total

strangers.

Jenny   48

when

there

is

nothing

appropriate

to be said,

offer

the gentle stroking

of your hand.

Helen   59

bad things seem to fall out of the sky.
but good things take work and time.

there is something so powerfully liberating about saying 'no, I'm sorry this isn't what I need to do right now.'

*f*launt
the imperfection

Domini 54

be the friend who is on call when others need you.

be willing to do the hard stuff.

Marlene   48

dad is special because he is the only person that lives in my house who has the same blood as me.

Mark 10

symbols of a survivor.
my scars
I wear proudly
as badges won in battle.

difficult journeys

can offer us the chance to learn
that we are loved and cared about.
I count myself fortunate to have
had this chance to know,
so clearly
and so strongly.

Kerry 59

the worst experiences
sometimes open
doors to the best
friendships.

Margie 53

even now

even the moon wanes
even the sun sets
stars ceased to glow
long ago

tides recede and
mountains slide
into seas

blossoms that scent the night
shroud the earth by dawn
and the heat of fierce embrace
fades in the glare of day

yet birds go berserk every morning
bursting their breasts with songs
as mourning mists drift away

and the sun rises
again and again
and again

and the sun

rises again

and again

and again